There's Always a Plan B

Charles Ray

U S
huru pres

North Potomac, MD

For information about this and other works of this author, contact the author at charlesray.author@yahoo.com.

Printed in the United States of America.

ISBN: 0615904408
ISBN-13: 978-0615904405 (Uhuru Press)

There's Always a Plan B

DEDICATION

To the people from whom I've learned all that I know about leadership throughout my life. But, especially to my grandmother, Sally Young, from whom I learned the most.

"The best laid plans of mice and men

Gang aft agley . . .

Robert Burns in 'To a Mouse', 1786

Introduction

During just over 20 years in the U.S. Army, July 1962 to September 1982, I learned many things. One of the most important things that I learned, though, after the main leadership principle of taking care of your people first, was the importance of planning. The army plans for everything. In fact, the military is constantly planning. Of course, the second thing I learned after the importance of planning was, the best battle plan doesn't survive the first shot.

Now, just what does that mean? And, if the plan is worthless when it comes time to execute, why bother with planning in the first place. Fair question, and one I hope the answer will be clear to by the time you finish reading this short book.

First, though, let me show you how I learned the importance of planning through decades of trial and error, and sometimes painful experience. In addition to my 20 years in uniform, I served over 30 years as a diplomat, a member of the U.S. Foreign Service, mostly abroad, and in some of our less desirable locations. During each of my tours, military or diplomatic, I encountered situations that were handled successfully, but had there not been advance planning, could easily have been disasters.

When I became U.S. Ambassador to Zimbabwe in 2009, at a time when relations between that country and the U.S. were a bit prickly, and the threat of general political violence was high, one of the early things I did was have my staff (known as the country team) review our Emergency Action Plan (EAP). The EAP is a document that is prepared by each of our diplomatic missions as a guide to dealing with a variety of different crises. Except in places where there are ongoing crises, like the Middle East, they are often ignored. Because there had been a fairly long interval with no violence in Zimbabwe, this was the case at the embassy in Harare.

Not only did I have the plan reviewed, but, working with my Regional Security Officer (RSO), I began to conduct exercises of various parts of the plan. We were shocked to discover that the overland evacuation route that had been part of the plan for years transited a region that was under the control of government hardliners with no love for the U.S., making an emergency evacuation of embassy employees and other American citizens problematical, if not downright dangerous. We began immediately to make adjustments, knowing that the day after we finished developing a plan it could very likely be rendered obsolete by a change in the political situation. But, the very fact that we were actively planning gave everyone a level of confidence that if the balloon went up, we would be able to cope.

Another example of the importance of planning was in Cambodia when I was ambassador there from 2002 to 2005. My RSO at that post was constantly exercising the guard force and making improvements, though minor, in the physical security of the mission. None of what we were able to do with the funds available would have withstood a determined assault, but the very fact of the planning activity saved us from disaster. We learned, after the fact, that an

Indonesian-based terrorist group had been conducting surveillance of the American and British embassies for a potential attack, and that the group had decided against attacking us because it was just too complicated to try and figure out a plan that would bypass all the planning and exercising we were doing.

I don't think I can put it any clearer than that, other than to say, planning is not done to give you a fixed list of actions to take when a situation arises. This is because every situation is different, and it's almost impossible to develop a plan that can be implemented exactly as written. But, planning forces you to think about all of the 'what-ifs' and it disciplines the mind, enabling you to respond more readily when things happen. Planning also ensure that everyone starts out with the same assumptions and from the same point, rather than reacting in a helter-skelter manner.

Another thing I learned over the years is that things will always go wrong. No matter how well you plan, or how easy a task seems, something will go awry, on that you can rely. The key to success, then, is not necessarily to have the perfectly executable plan, but to achieve your goal despite the fact that things don't go as you planned. An old army sergeant with whom I worked years ago said, when things don't go as you anticipate, and most of the time they won't, just remember that there's always 'Plan B.'

I hope that by the time you reach the end of this book, you too will always keep in mind that, when things start to fall apart with your original plan of action, there's no need to sweat. You knew at the start that it was likely to happen, and you're prepared. You'll just switch to Plan B.

There's Always a Plan B

Charles Ray

1. Why It's Important to Have a Plan

Undertaking a new task without having done at least some advance planning is like going for a trek in a strange forest without a map; it's a good way to get lost before you even start.

A prime historical example of the danger of starting a task without a good plan in hand is American experience in World War I. Due to a lack of peacetime training and planning by the army, American casualties were high, and it was a year after the U.S. declaration of war before troops were even minimally ready to be sent into combat.

George Catlett Marshall, who was only a captain at that time, saw the need for continuous planning, and in fact, when later he was an instructor at the army's infantry school at Ft. Benning, Georgia, stressed to his students the need to 'study the first six months of the *next* war (emphasis mine).' Marshall's philosophy was that planning in advance was the time to try things out, and if they didn't work, find out what's needed to make them work.

Careful, deliberate planning helps you see potential obstacles before they appear to trip you up, and allow mitigating actions to be developed. Marshall, in fact, believed that in planning, the country had to be prepared to meet the worst situation that might develop. His planning philosophy was as follows:

- Identify all potential crisis scenarios

- Prepare to deal with them

- Develop a monitoring and reporting system to assess your progress

- Train to your plan

- Get feedback at every step in the process

The first consideration in developing a plan is the ultimate goal, but the process of identifying potential stumbling blocks or crises is equally important. As my grandmother always said when I was growing up, prepare for the worst and hope for the best.

When potential problems have been identified, the next step is to map out ways to solve them, or turn them to advantage.

A system to measure progress and provide that information to everyone involved in a plan's implementation should an integral part of the plan.

Organizations need to develop training and exercise programs (that's right, it's not just the military that needs training, folks) to test plans. Training should be based on real world conditions if it is to be relevant and useful.

Getting feedback in every step of the planning process from all stakeholders and participants not only increases potential for positive input, but helps to ensure buy-in for the implementation phase.

"Expect the best, plan for the worst, and prepare to be surprised," – Denis Waitley

One can see an example of what happens when there hasn't been adequate planning was the situation facing U.S. forces after the fall of Baghdad in 2003. Having gone in against Saddam Hussein's forces with no clear post-conflict plan, the U.S. was unprepared for the massive looting and destruction of public facilities and the subsequent sectarian violence that threatened to undermine the whole operation.

In summary, having a plan helps in identifying potential problem areas, and ensures that everyone at least starts the job from the same basic position. There's an old army saying, 'the best war plan doesn't survive the first shot,' recognizing that the future has a perverse way of turning left when we'd planned to go right. But, a weak plan, or a plan that has to be radically altered to fit a changed situation is far better than having no plan at all.

Charles Ray

There's Always a Plan B

2. But, a Plan Should Never Be a Straitjacket

Having a plan of action is important, but the plan is only a guide, a starting point if you will. Once you're underway, it's essential to be prepared to make adjustments to fit the situation you face. Following a plan to the letter, in the face of changed circumstances, is like continuing down a road marked on your map, even though you've observed that the bridge is out ahead, and you're heading for a precipice; it's a recipe for sure disaster.

There are two kinds of people I hate dealing with; the kind who never plan anything, and who're always caught with their pants down when the inevitable crisis hits; and, the 'by the book' types who are incapable of making adjustments when it's as clear as a pimple on prom night that the plan isn't working.

The problem with the first type, people who face

life with no plan, is that often, they also have no clear vision of their goal, haven't a clue as to the potential roadblocks that are apt to get in their way; for whom *every* setback quickly becomes a crisis. They are forever lurching from one crisis to the next, never making any discernible progress toward an often equally indiscernible goal.

The second type, though, is even more frustrating. Having developed a plan, far too often, the *plan* becomes the objective, and the original goal for which the plan was developed becomes subordinate, if it doesn't disappear in its entirety.

In bureaucracies, the content of plans all often become the rules by which the bureaucracy operates, and anyone who has had experience with such organizations knows that bureaucrats live by rules. Compliance with 'rules' becomes the goal. In such situations, the original goal of an organization can get lost, and to me, that's a sure road to frustration.

I encountered an example of 'follow the rules, and damn the consequences' when I was ambassador to Cambodia. Upon arrival in the country, I learned that, because of certain political attitudes in Washington, we were restricted in our ability to deal directly with the police and military units responsible for Cambodia's border security. As this was in the wake of the catastrophic 9/11 attacks, and we knew that there were radical Muslim groups in Southeast Asia that sympathized with al Qaeda, this made no sense to me.

After consultations with my defense attaché and other officials in country, as well as the regional military command, I made a proposal that we modify the rules to allow us to get real-time information from border security units, and be able to provide them the necessary training to enable them to do a better job. Needless to say, the response back from the civilian bureaucracy was, 'not now, it breaks rules, written and unwritten, on what contact is allowed.' I let this untenable situation go on until I began to learn that there had in fact been terrorist activity that we didn't learn about until it was too late, and that we'd been spared an attack only through incredibly good luck.

My final action was to use my authority as the president's representative to go around the bureaucracy and directly to senior decision makers – something a career diplomat does as a last resort because of the potential for career backlash. To me, though, taking action to prevent loss of American lives was more important than keeping a bunch of red-tape wielding pencil pushers happy.

The result of my action, as I'd anticipated, was an immediate cry for my head from those up and down the bureaucratic chain. Fortunately, the senior decision makers saw the merit in what I proposed, and stepped in to stem the flow of criticism. The policy was changed as I recommended, and eventually the bureaucracy developed new rules (a new plan) to accord with the new reality. But, it took a bit of head-knocking to get them to do it.

A plan, like a rule, is a guide. It should be followed under normal circumstances. But, when the situation you face has clearly changed from what it was when the plan or rule was developed, then it's time to use your brain, and figure out what really *needs* to be done to achieve your goal, not blindly follow a plan or rule that just might be OBE (overtaken by events).

"No battle plan ever survived contact with the enemy." Source unknown, but sometimes credited to General Von Moltke, Bismarck's chief of staff in the Franco-Prussian War

---

Charles Ray

There's Always a Plan B

3. The Importance of Thinking Positively

It might not be self-evident, but a critically important element in successful planning, or any other endeavor for that matter, is a positive attitude.

"If you think you can, you might be wrong, but if you think you can't, you'll be right every time."
– My grandmother

Now what, you might ask, does thinking positively have to do with constructing plans?

Consider this. You're deeply immersed in the planning process. You're at the point where you're considering all the potential crises that can crop up (remember George C. Marshall's steps from chapter 1?). If you're the 'glass half full' type, the first crisis you envision will throw you into a complete tizzy. If not the first, certainly the second, because you see, you'll be convinced that this means your goal is unachievable. Don't believe me? Think about how many times you've seen people refuse to try something new because they're convinced they can't do it.

Negativity is a self-fulfilling prophecy. When you take a dim view of life, it's pretty hard to see your way clearly enough to make the most of opportunities that come your way. A positive attitude, on the other hand, can increase your level of productivity, and it can help you see the bright side of even a bad situation. Comes in handy as you're in that phase of planning where you're looking at potential crisis scenarios if you can approach them with a 'can-overcome' attitude, don't you think?

Maintaining a positive outlook also helps you to build the necessary relationships of trust and confidence with colleagues that are essential to success in any endeavor. It can help you feel better and live better, which in the long run, is also necessary if the success you're working toward is to be enjoyed.

4. Dealing With Brick Walls and Stumbling Blocks

Every organization has them; in every situation you'll encounter them. These are the brick walls and stumbling blocks of people whose default answer is 'no,' or the situations that are like the *Kobiyashi Maru* scenario in the *Star Trek*™ universe – unsolvable – or at least, seemingly unsolvable.

For those of you unfamiliar with *Star Trek*, the scenario mentioned was designed to be an unsolvable no-win situation in order to test the ability of the Star Fleet Academy cadets to deal in situations where they had to persevere, even in the face of insurmountable odds or certain defeat. In the highly successful TV/movie/book series created by Gene Roddenberry, James Tiberius Kirk, who went on to captain the starship *Enterprise*, beat the *Kobiyashi Maru* scenario by sneaking into the school and reprogramming the computer. His reasoning; "I don't believe in no-win situations," the character playing him in the movie said nonchalantly.

That, my friend, has to be you when you're planning and implementing your plans. No-win situations are for losers, and you don't want to be a loser, do you?

"Take 'no' as an interim answer." Deputy Secretary of State Richard Armitage in a conversation with the author in 2004.

When I served as American ambassador to Cambodia, I saw the need to alter a policy that had been put into place for valid reasons at the time it was implemented, but that had been overtaken by events in the interim, and had, in fact, become dangerous. The bureaucracy, however, is always more comfortable 'doing it the way it's always been done,' and the answer to my request for a policy review was a wobbly 'no'; by which I mean, the bureaucrats came back with 'the time's not right, let's wait a while.' If you've ever worked in a bureaucracy, you'll know, this is a way of saying 'no' without actually having to say, 'no.'

I put up with this for a few months, until I realized that letting the pencil pushers get away with this ploy was exposing my staff to danger. I then did what was a bureaucratic 'no-no'; I went straight to the top, bypassing all the minions who had inserted themselves into my chain of communication, and made the recommendation to the two men who had the power to decide, the secretaries of defense and state. Now, this wasn't strictly a violation of the rules, but it violated the bureaucratically imposed 'protocols' whereby an ambassador communicates through his bureau and country desk. Thing is, ambassadors are appointed by the president, and are authorized to communicate with anyone in the executive branch. This didn't keep the pencil pushers from screaming to high heaven, demanding my head for such a gross violation of bureaucratic etiquette.

It was only when Rich Armitage, then-deputy secretary of state, stepped in and put his foot down hard, that the yowling and baying stopped. His view was that I'd done what I was authorized to do, and what, under the circumstances, was the prudent thing to do. He then reminded the howling bureaucrats that if I should overstep my authority, he or the secretary of state would fire me. I wasn't being fired for doing what I thought was right, rather than waiting for instructions. He then turned to me and said, "Always take more authority than you think you're really entitled to, and wait for someone in higher authority to tell you to desist, and always take 'no' for an interim answer." That was the end of that meeting, and I never had a chance to talk to him after that, but those words have forever stuck in my mind.

My 50 years in the bureaucracy taught me that there are two main kinds of people, those who say 'no' as soon as you ask them for something, hoping that you'll go away and leave the status quo intact, and those who say, 'let me see what I can do,' and who look for ways to get the job done despite the restrictions of rules and tradition. My concern is that there are probably more of the former than the latter, because saying 'no' rarely gets a person into trouble, while taking initiative, can, as my previous example illustrates, bring the wrath of the bureaucracy down upon your head.

So, what do you as a planner do about the naysayers and brick walls in your organization? It would be nice if you could just ignore them, hoping they'd go away, but, alas, that's seldom possible. The best planning is done when you involve all stakeholders in the organization to some degree; and, the roadblocks are stakeholders, albeit stakeholders who want to prevent change, as much as anyone else. Here are a few things that have worked for me over the years:

- Identify the people in your organization who are most resistant to change.

- Involve them early, but in a limited way, with plans for change.

- Get their feedback. Sometimes, even though they resist change, they can come up with input that help make a plan better, and letting them do so can get buy-in from all but the most resistant to change.

- When they pose objections, insist that they explain why, and come up with alternative solutions. Don't allow them to just say 'no'.

This method doesn't always work; some people are just too resistant to change. In those cases, you have to either find a way to work around them, or, if you're in charge, consider removing them.

Decades ago, when I was assigned as a Foreign Service administrative officer at a consulate general in Southeast Asia, I inherited a situation that begged for immediate change; change that was resisted by, of all people, the man at the top – my boss. We had a small post office that operated under the rules of the military postal service, rules that are as stringent as the U.S. Post Office. Break them, and you can lose your mail privileges, and in extreme cases, even be prosecuted for violation of federal law.

Well, in this case, I discovered that when the mail bag came in at the local airport, an employee from my section picked it up, brought it to the consulate general, and left it opened in a room behind my secretary's desk. American staff then came in and dug through the bag to find their mail. I don't think I have to tell you that this was a gross violation of mail regulations, and a dangerous thing to do.

The chance of mail being lost or stolen was a risk I wasn't prepared to take, so I had a contractor install mailboxes with locks for each section, individual or family in the consulate general, and issued them the keys with an announcement that henceforth all mail would be kept secure, and, except for me, my secretary, and the driver, only the addressee would have access. A few people grumbled at having to remember to bring their mailbox key to work, but my boss flew into a mini-rage over it. I was really afraid that he might even ask the State Department to remove me from post. I finally made a deal with him; I'd keep his key, and even though it wasn't exactly within regulations, I'd retrieve his mail from the mailroom (next to my office) and deliver it to his desk. That placated him, and things eventually quieted down, but it just goes to show that you can manage naysayers with a little finesse and luck, even when they're senior to you in the pecking order; you just have to be willing to take a little heat.

5. Starting at the End

In discussions of getting things done, you will most often here that it's always best to start at the beginning and work through to the end. In fact, in my first book on leadership, *Things I Learned from My Grandmother About Leadership and Life*, I stressed this, and gave an example of something my grandmother often said, "start reading a book on page one."

Now, this is good advice, but planning is an exception to the rule. Because the goal or objective you're setting out to accomplish is the most important element of your plan; it is after all the reason you're planning in the first place; a good place to begin your planning is at the very end.

"Setting goals is the first step in turning the invisible into the visible." Tony Robbins

Reverse planning, or developing a plan from the objective back to the starting point, is commonly used in project management. This technique, however, is quite useful in any kind planning, from a military operation to how to organize a yard sale.

A plan that is well thought out improves the chances of the desired goal being reached. Whether in the workplace of our personal lives, failure to plan is planning to fail. Often, people don't take the time to plan because they're not sure of their goals, or they are so caught up in the minutiae of day-to-day live, they don't take the time to step back from the details and look at the long view. This is a mistake.

Once you realize that taking the time to plan is time well-spent, the next question is; what is the most effective way to go about planning? I am a firm believer that planning from the desired end-state backwards is far superior to most other methods.

Here are the planning steps in this method:

- Identify and clearly define your goal.

- Delineate each step needed to attain your goal.

- Create a timeline to reach your goal.

- Identify critical points along your timeline, including potential setbacks, and create alternatives.

- Identify and seek the support needed to reach your goal.

Following is an example of how planning from your goal backwards, as well as some of the other principles discussed to this point, work in actual practice.

In early 2013, a friend had invited me to visit West Africa as part of a media delegation. I was more than happy to oblige, but a bit concerned that he was in charge of all arrangements, including getting our visas to enter the country we were visiting. This meant that I had to give him my passport. I'm never comfortable doing that; and that feeling was validated when, on the day we were due to travel, he decided to go to a dentist's appointment.

I got to the airport in plenty of time, but he didn't make it, with our passports, until five minutes after the flight closed.

Now, at this point, most people would have thrown their hands up in disgust. We'd missed our flight to Paris where we were to connect with a flight to our final destination. That is, in fact, what he did. I, on the other hand, decided that before we gave up and went home, our plans for the trip in the trash, we should look for Plan B.

We went to the airline counter, explained our situation, and I asked if there was any way we might be able to be put on another flight that would get us to Paris in time to catch the flight we were scheduled to depart on from there. Turned out, there was, and not only were we rebooked, but I managed to talk the clerk out of charging us for it – who said airlines can't be flexible. We got to Paris, made our connection, and the trip was a success.

What the heck does that have to do with planning, you ask? Well, it just goes to show that if you plan for success, and follow the principles I've outlined so far, you can overcome adversity. You can make things work, even when your original plan goes off track. Here's the outline of the trip following the guidelines we've discussed:

- Goal: Get to West Africa on time to meet the delegation

- Potential Problems: Missed flight

- Work Around: Find alternate flight, talk our way onto the flight, keep a positive attitude, and seek support

- Result: Plan A went south because my friend didn't plan his time properly, but thanks to Plan B we still achieved our goal.

It's that simple. The next time you're faced with a situation when it seems the wheels are coming off, stop, take a deep breath, and consider Plan B.

6. A Straight Line is Not Always the Shortest Route to Your Destination

In geometry, a straight line is the shortest distance between two points. In life, however, a straight line is not always the quickest way to get from one point to another.

From the time of our birth until we breathe our last, from the moment we wake up in the morning until we go to sleep at night, we are faced with choices, we must make decisions, we come to forks in the road. Geometry aside, life does not proceed in a straight line.

> **"If you can see your path laid out in front of you step by step, you know it's not your path. Your own path you make with every step you take."**
> **Joseph Campbell**

In planning, whether for a major business initiative, or simply what to do for the coming weekend, keep in mind that, while you will endeavor to develop a plan that will get you to your objective in the shortest time possible, the most effective and successful way might not be the most direct.

As you assess potential roadblocks to achieving your goal, you must also develop ways to deal with them. When you encounter an obstacle, you have a number of choices:

- Remove it. Go through it.

- Minimize it. Go over, around, or under it.

- Ignore it. Find an alternate route: Plan B

-   Be stopped by it.

Some obstacles are merely minor nuisances, and can be easily overcome. A subordinate who is always late for work can, if he refuses to improve, be dismissed or reassigned. Some are more significant; requiring more effort to deal with. In the case of the bureaucracy that blocked my efforts to get a policy change when I was ambassador to Cambodia, for instance, it was impossible to remove them from the board, but I was able to use an alternate channel of communication to bypass them entirely. There will be times, though, when you have to take a step or two back, and find a completely new route to your objective. I faced such a situation in Zimbabwe when an office in Washington wanted me to make a public statement on one issue that could have created danger for an American citizen who was completely uninvolved with the issue at hand. It was a risky thing to do, but I basically ignored that office, and did something entirely different. In the end, the American's problem was resolved amicably, and the issue that had bureaucrats in Washington spun up turned out to be a non-issue that resolved itself.

As to being stopped by a problem; I include

this because some people do, in fact, allow stumbling blocks to become impenetrable barriers to goal accomplishment. When they encounter a problem or crisis, they become frozen; unsure of what to do next. All forward progress comes to a halt. All I have to say about that is: don't be one of these people.

Charles Ray

There's Always a Plan B

7. A Few Closing Words

How long should a book on planning be? Should it be hundreds or thousands of pages long, filled with graphs, charts, and summaries of research studies? Or, should it be just enough to get you to thinking about how you go about planning, just long enough to get your creative juices flowing?

"How long should a man's legs be? Long enough to reach the ground." J.D. Salinger

---

What I hope I have imparted to you in this brief book is the importance of planning, in your personal *and* professional life, because if you fail to plan you are planning to fail. More importantly, though, I hope I have convinced you that you need to have a flexible approach to planning.

If there is one thing in life that is as certain as death and taxes, it is that things will often go wrong. When they do, however, it doesn't mean that you can't achieve your goals – it must means that you have to take another path to your objective. Remember; there is always a Plan B.

Other books on leadership and management by this author

THINGS I LEARNED FROM MY
GRANDMOTHER ABOUT
LEADERSHIP AND LIFE

(How to Light a Fire Under People
Without Burning Them Out)

CHARLES RAY

There are thousands of books in print that discuss leadership, but Charles Ray, a successful leader of government organizations (military and civilian) for over forty years, believes that there was need for one that addresses leadership from a practitioner's viewpoint. *Things I Learned from My Grandmother About Leadership and Life* is that book.

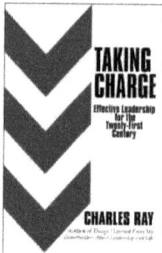

TAKING CHARGE

Effective Leadership
for the
Twenty-First
Century

CHARLES RAY

In the turbulent twenty-first century, we need enlightened leadership more than ever before. In board rooms and in command centers, from the White House to each state house, we need leaders who are focused on getting the job done. In *Taking Charge*, Charles Ray offers the Principles that give us that leadership..

Those who dare take chances are often the most successful. Charles Ray, through examples from his own life, talks about the importance of thinking and acting outside the box in his third book on practical leadership.

These books are available online from Amazon.com and other retail book sites. They can also be purchased through the store link at the author's Web site http://charlesaray.blogspot.com.

Charles Ray

About the Author

Charles Ray has been writing fiction since his teens. He won a Sunday school magazine writing contest when he was thirteen, and having his byline on a short story published in a national publication forever hooked him on writing. During his time in the army (1962-1982) he often moonlighted as a newspaper or magazine journalist, and was the editorial cartoonist for the Spring Lake (NC) News, a weekly newspaper, during the 1970s. In addition to his writing, he was an artist/cartoonist and photographer for a number of publications, including Ebony, Eagle and Swan, and Essence, and had a monthly cartoon feature and did several covers for Buffalo, a now-defunct magazine that was dedicated to showcasing the contributions of African-Americans to the country's military history.

After retiring from the army, he joined the U.S. Foreign Service, and served as a diplomat in posts in Asia and Africa until his retirement in 2012. He has worked and traveled throughout the world (Antarctica is the only continent he hasn't visited), and now, as a full time writer, continues to globetrot looking for interesting things to write about, draw, or take pictures of.

A native of Texas, he now calls Maryland home. For more on his writing and other projects, check one of the following Web sites:

http://redroom.com/member/charles-a-ray
http://charlesaray.blogspot.com
http://charlieray45.wordpress.com
http://www.twitter.com/charlieray45
http://www.facebook.com/charlieray45
http://www.flickr.com/photos/charlesray45/
http://www.viewbug.com/member/charlesray

www.ingramcontent.com/pod-product-compliance
Lightning Source LLC
Chambersburg PA
CBHW071336200326
41520CB00013B/3007